A Robbie Reader

Gardening For Kids

A Kid's Guide to Perennial Gardens

Tamra Orr

Mitchell Lane
PUBLISHERS

P.O. Box 196
Hockessin, Delaware 19707
Visit us on the web: www.mitchelllane.com
Comments? email us: mitchelllane@mitchelllane.com

Gardening For Kids

A Backyard Flower Garden for Kids

A Backyard Vegetable Garden for Kids

Design Your Own Butterfly Garden

Design Your Own Pond and Water Garden

A Kid's Guide to Landscape Design

A Kid's Guide to Perennial Gardens

Copyright © 2009 by Mitchell Lane Publishers

ABOUT THE AUTHOR: Tamra Orr is the author of more than 100 nonfiction books for kids of all ages, including titles about fire ants, presidents and their childhoods, test-tube babies, astronauts, and the Salem witch trials. When she isn't writing or researching, she is enjoying the beauty of the Pacific Northwest. She likes to spend time outside in the backyard, gardening with her three children. She is known not only for naming her plants, but for carrying on entire monologues for their benefit. Orr credits her mother-in-law for teaching her about gardening; Orr was introduced to the concept of planting, weeding, harvesting, and then cooking food by her husband's mother.

PUBLISHER'S NOTE: The facts on which the story in this book is based have been thoroughly researched. Documentation of such research can be found on page 46. While every possible effort has been made to ensure accuracy, the publisher will not assume liability for damages caused by inaccuracies in the data, and makes no warranty on the accuracy of the information contained herein.

Library of Congress Cataloging-in-Publication Data
Orr, Tamra.
  A kid's guide to perennial gardens / by Tamra Orr.
    p. cm. — (Robbie reader. Gardening for kids)
  Includes bibliographical references and index.
    ISBN 978-1-58415-636-9 (library bound)
    1. Perennials—Juvenile literature.
2. Gardening—Juvenile literature. I. Title. II. Series.
  SB434.O77 2008
  635.9'32—dc22
                                    2008002254

Printing   1   2   3   4   5   6   7   8   9

                                              PLB

Contents

Words in **bold** type can be found in the glossary.

Introduction

One of the most beautiful summer sights is a flower garden in bloom. When it is bursting with color, it can look like a rainbow that has been trapped on the ground. Gardening is a way to bring nature into your life, even if it is just in a small pot or a window box. Through gardening, you can connect to the soil and the sun.

Before you start any project, talk to your parents. Ask them what they think of the idea of putting in a garden. Do they have any tips for you? Perhaps they even want to help you. Remember, it is important

that you have their permission before you dig a single hole!

When creating a garden, keep in mind where you live. How much rain do you get? Does the sun shine often? There is a map in this book that will help you pinpoint your climate zone (see page 11). Knowing what zone you live in will help your garden grow stronger and healthier.

Making a garden is fun, and it can inspire some fun crafts too. Enjoy everything—from the digging and planting to the growing and creating. A perennial garden is going to be with you for several years. It will give you the chance to invent your own personal rainbow.

Chapter

1

Taking Time to Plan

Like any other project, perennial gardening takes planning. Imagine you are taking a trip to another city, state, or even country. Even though you might think the first step for this adventure is throwing together your favorite clothes and stuffing your backpack with snacks and a few books (not to mention leaving a note to say where you're going!), there are some questions you have to answer first:

Where are you going?
How are you going to get there?
How much will it cost?
What supplies do you need?
How long will it take?
What do you want to do on the way—and when you arrive?
Will you need any help on the trip?

By figuring out all these details first, your trip will most likely bring you more fun than problems. The same is true for planting a garden. It is a fun thing to do, but it takes some planning before the planting!

Before you grab a shovel and start digging a hole in the backyard, inspired by pictures in your head of a beautiful garden, you need to do some homework about perennial gardens.

A perennial garden is like your very own rainbow on the ground. There may not be a pot of gold, but you get to keep it all summer long and it will come back again next year!

What Is a Perennial, Anyway?

Perennials make a bright, exciting garden. They usually have colorful showy or **ornamental** flowers. The word *perennial* means "lasting" or "enduring." The word comes from the Latin word *perennis,* which means "throughout the years." When it comes to

Common Types of Perennial Plants and What Amount of Sunshine They Need to Grow

FULL SUN	PARTIAL SHADE	FULL SHADE
Anemone	Geranium	Lily of the Valley
Aster	Monkshood	Jack-in-the-Pulpit
Iris	Columbine	Wild Ginger
Peony	Foxglove	Lungwort
Poppy	Meadow Rue	Toad Lily

gardening, the term refers to plants and flowers that bloom for one season, go **dormant** or inactive over the winter, and then return again the next spring—and the next and the next and the next. *Annual* gardening, on the other hand, refers to planting flowers that grow for one season and then, after going to seed, do not come back. A spring annual blooms in the spring, a summer annual in summer, and so on. *Biennial* gardening means growing plants that take two years to flower, which then die that second year.

Perennials are not called "immortal" or "forever," though. They may last two, four, or six years before they finally fade away. Because they come back, they usually take less work over time, especially for a first-time gardener.

Watching the Weather

Have you ever paid much attention to the weather? Have you thought about how often it rains and at what time of the year? Have you considered how

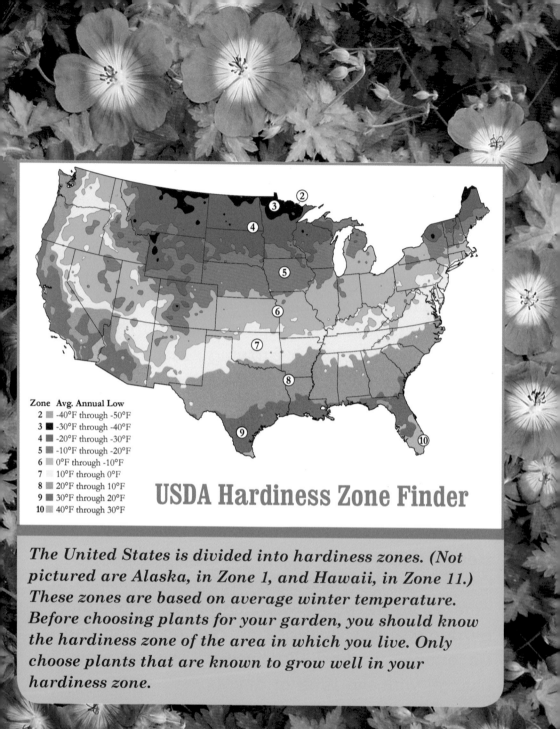

Zone Avg. Annual Low
2 ▨ -40°F through -50°F
3 ■ -30°F through -40°F
4 ▨ -20°F through -30°F
5 ▨ -10°F through -20°F
6 ▨ 0°F through -10°F
7 ▨ 10°F through 0°F
8 ▨ 20°F through 10°F
9 ▨ 30°F through 20°F
10 ▨ 40°F through 30°F

USDA Hardiness Zone Finder

The United States is divided into hardiness zones. (Not pictured are Alaska, in Zone 1, and Hawaii, in Zone 11.) These zones are based on average winter temperature. Before choosing plants for your garden, you should know the hardiness zone of the area in which you live. Only choose plants that are known to grow well in your hardiness zone.

much sunshine you get in the summer and how much shade? If you start your own garden, weather details will become more important to you.

Knowing what the summer and fall climate or weather is like where you live is very important. Some plants and flowers do well in some areas and terrible in others. Use the climate zone map, known as the USDA Hardiness Zone Finder, to figure out what your zone is. This map was developed by the U.S. Department of Agriculture to help gardeners make the most of their growing season.

The lower 48 United States are divided into nine different zones. Each zone is 10 degrees Fahrenheit warmer or colder than the zone next to it. Most seed catalogs and nurseries follow this map when they list their plants, and they note the best climates for each one.

Keeping Track

Once you know what climate zone you are in, it is time to figure out how much shade and sun your garden will get. Just looking now and then will not be enough to find the answer. The amounts will change with the time of day as well as the time of year. To get enough information to start, however, you might create a chart like this one. At each time of day, fill in whether your garden area is getting

Time	Week 1	Week 2	Week 3	Week 4	Week 5	Week 6
8 A.M.						
Noon						
4 P.M.						

full shade, partial shade, partial sun, or full sun. Do this for more than one part of the yard so that you'll know the best places to plant.

Take a few weeks to fill out your chart and get a good idea of how much sun and shade your garden is likely to get throughout the day. Note where the shadows fall at each time of day, and jot down how many hours seem to be spent in full sun, partial shade, and full shade. This information will help you make the right choices for your plants.

Now that you have a better idea of the amounts of sun and shade, you will know where to plant which flowers or plants.

Chapter

Chapter

2

Putting Plans on Paper

You're well on your way to an amazing garden. You know what a perennial is; now it is time to find out what these plants look like and how they grow. Why is this important? If you just scatter seeds into your garden without any idea of what they will grow into, you will probably regret it. The tall plants will cover up the short ones. They may all bloom at once and then be finished for the rest of the summer. The colors may clash. A high-sun flower may be right next to one that needs shade. A pretty garden does not just happen—it takes some careful planning.

Start by going online, stopping by a local nursery, or ordering a flower seed catalog to find out what plants and flowers are available. Look through the examples and see which perennials you like the best. Make sure the ones you choose are able to grow well in your climate zone. If your yard or window box gets only a few hours of sun each day, you will need plants that like shade. On the other hand, if your area is in full sun for most of each day, you will want to choose flowers that grow best in a lot of sun.

As you go, make a list of the names of flowers you like, and then fill out a chart with the following information:

> Name
> Color
> How tall they grow
> When they bloom
> How much sunlight and shade they need
> What kind of soil they need

You also have to know how much space you have to work with before you can order your flowers. If you are working with a window box or even just a few clay pots, you will order a lot fewer plants than if your parents have allowed you a large portion of the yard. Fortunately, seeds do not cost very much, usually between $1 and $3 per packet, and each packet contains anywhere from 30 to 200 seeds.

As you plan out your garden, you might want to stop by a local nursery to see what the plants will look like as they grow. Most nurseries have potted perennials that you can see and even use in your own garden.

Next, get a piece of graph paper and begin drawing the plan for your garden. Map out the area you have available. If it is outside, be sure to include any trees, bushes, fences, or sidewalks that are in the same area. Also, be sure to pick an area that is easy for you to get to.

Garden Tip

What style of garden do you want? Experts say that flowers in red, pink, blue, and purple shades tend to cool or soften the look of a garden. On the other hand, orange and yellow brighten it up.

You want to be able to reach all sides of it for watering and weeding. Be sure to avoid places that never get any sun or any shade. A mix of sun and shade is often best.

Before you start drawing on your graph paper, carefully measure how much room you have. How many feet and inches long and wide will your garden be? Transfer the shape onto your map. Figure out a workable scale, such as "one inch on paper is equal to one foot outside."

Remember to organize your plants with the tallest ones in back. If you put them in front, they will block your view of the smaller ones. Also think about which colors you want next to each other. Try to choose a variety of flowers that bloom at different times throughout the spring, summer, and even

Taking time to draw your plans on paper is an important step. Just as you wouldn't go on a long journey without a map, you don't want to start a garden without a well-planned diagram.

early fall. That way, your garden will always have some color in it.

At last, your planning is done. It's time to take your ideas off paper and into the dirt!

Chapter

Chapter

3

Preparing the Soil, Planting the Seeds

At last your diagram is drawn, your seed packets have arrived, and you are ready to start planting your garden. Take a glance at the calendar. What time of year is it? The best months for planting seeds in most areas of the United States are June and July. The soil has had a chance to warm up by then.

What if you want to plant earlier? One of the best ways to get your plants started is by putting them in small containers like pots, milk cartons, or trays. This is often called **container planting.** If done properly, it gives your plants a strong beginning. By the time you transfer the plants to the garden outside, they will already have a healthy root system.

Indoor planting can be done in April and May. To get started, gather some simple supplies, including:

Potting soil
Seed packets or containers of
    perennials from the store
Clay pots or other containers
Simple, small rocks
Trowel(s)
Watering can

Begin by placing some rocks at the bottom of your pot to help with water **drainage**. The rocks will support the soil, yet allow the water to drain through the hole in the bottom of the pot. If your pots are inside, be sure to place a saucer under them to catch excess water.

Next, using the trowel, fill the pot with soil up to one inch from the top.

Place the seeds in the dirt, then lightly cover them with soil. If the seeds come in a seed packet, look on the back and follow its directions very carefully. Commonly, perennials will come in one-, five-, and even fifteen-gallon containers. They often have directions on the side also.

Next, add water to the soil.

Place the pots where they will get sunshine each day, and check them every other day to see if they have enough water. Soon, the first green shoots will pop through the top of the dirt, and your garden will have begun!

Garden Tip

If you would like to know exactly what your soil is missing, you can take a sample of it into your local county extension office for testing. Be sure to grab a sample that is six to eight inches down from the surface. The service will provide a report (usually free of charge) of what your soil needs to be healthier.

Preparing the Soil

While your plants are getting a good head start inside, you can work on improving the soil where they will be transferred. The better the soil, the better your plants will grow.

First, remove all grass, weeds, and anything else growing in the area you are going to plant. Turn the soil over: Exposing dirt to sun is a great way to kill any possible diseases lurking in it. After it has dried in the sun, which typically takes at least 12 hours of sunshine, cover it with a black plastic tarp, available in local nurseries or hardware stores. Anchor the corners with rocks so that it will not blow off in the

Putting a tarp on top of your soil will help the dirt get warm and stay warm. When you finally take the tarp off, the soil will be healthier and ready for planting.

Preparing your soil before you put any seeds or plants into it is a very important step. Imagine moving into a place that did not have enough food for you to eat or water to drink. It would not be good for you—and you'd feel miserable. It's the same for your plants. Their new home in your garden soil should be full of the nutrients they need. It should also be easy for you to reach so that you can keep it weeded and watered.

wind. Leave the tarp on for a few weeks or up to two months. As the sun shines down on it and the plastic heats up, the temperature of the soil will also rise. This kills **bacteria**.

If your soil looks pale and seems sandy, you will need to make it healthier. There are several ways to do this. You can buy **fertilizer** and, following the directions, **have an adult help you** add it to the dirt. You can also add **organic** material to give the soil the **nutrients** and minerals it needs. Organic material includes natural things like grass clippings, straw, and leaves. One of the best ways to make the soil richer is to add a thick layer of **mulch** to keep moisture in and weeds out.

Mulch helps to keep away insects and protects soil from being washed away by rain. Mulch can be made out of many different things, including newspapers, cardboard, manure, shredded bark, sawdust, and wool.

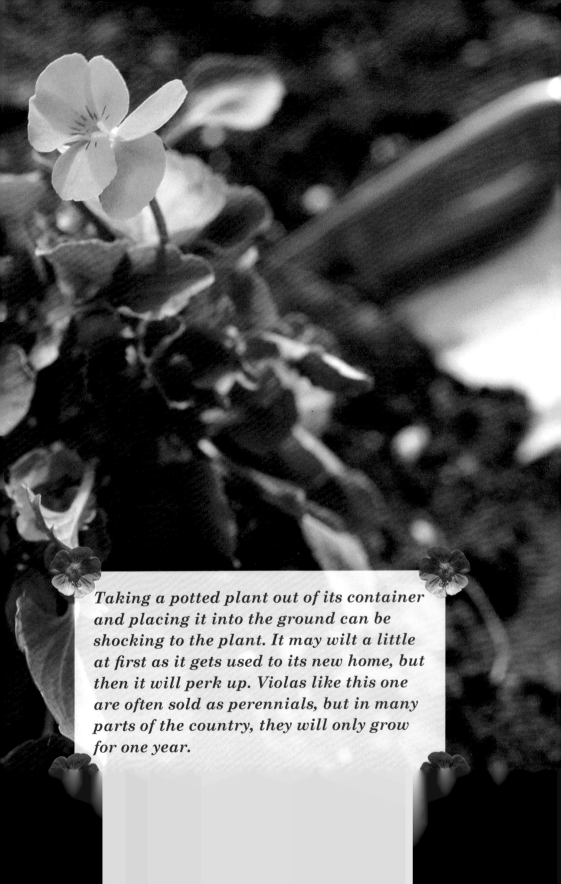

Taking a potted plant out of its container and placing it into the ground can be shocking to the plant. It may wilt a little at first as it gets used to its new home, but then it will perk up. Violas like this one are often sold as perennials, but in many parts of the country, they will only grow for one year.

As summer begins, your soil should be healthier and your seeds already on the way to becoming flowers and plants. When it comes time to move your plants from their individual containers to the garden, do it carefully. Tap the side of the container lightly to loosen the dirt. Pull the plant out by its base, making sure to do so gently. Shake some of the dirt loose, and then place the plant into the hole you have ready for it in the garden.

How close should you plant them? In groups of three or five, the general rule of thumb is:

Tall plants	18 to 36 inches apart
Intermediate plants	12 to 18 inches apart
Dwarf or small plants	6 to 12 inches apart

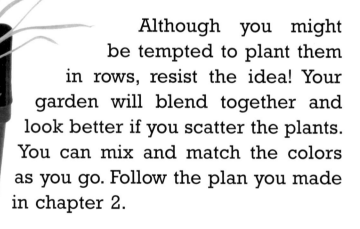

Although you might be tempted to plant them in rows, resist the idea! Your garden will blend together and look better if you scatter the plants. You can mix and match the colors as you go. Follow the plan you made in chapter 2.

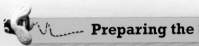

Remember that some of the steps in planting a garden need an adult's help. Spending time together outside creating a rainbow for your family can be a fun project for everyone.

Finally, step back and admire your work. Your rainbow is on its way!

4

Taking Care of Your Garden

Creating a perennial garden takes a lot of patience. The first year that you plant everything, your garden is just getting started. It begins to fill in. The second year, it is established and comes in thicker and stronger. The third year is considered the best one of all. By this time, everything is filled out and complete. Take pictures! This is a perennial garden at its best.

During the summer and fall, there is not a lot of work to be done on your garden. The most important steps are as follows:

Keeping your garden watered. Check your garden every three or four days throughout the season. If it is extremely hot where you live or you have a hot spell, you may have to water every day or every other day for a while. You will know if your plants or flowers are low on water if their leaves are drooping and their blossoms begin to drop. Water early in the morning or late in the evening.

Keeping weeds out. About once a week, go through your garden and check for weeds. They grow fast and are sneaky! If you spot one, pull it out. Make sure you get the roots and not just the part of the plant above the soil level. You want to make sure they are picked before they have the chance to spread or go to seed. Many gardeners use a type of **herbicide**, or weed killer, to help control the unwanted species. These often contain dangerous or toxic chemicals. Some companies offer natural alternatives made from materials like baking soda and sulfur.

Keeping insects under control. Certain kinds of bugs can destroy a garden, so it is important to keep them under control. Some of the worst ones to have in your garden include sow bugs and pill bugs, spider mites, earwigs, and aphids. You will need a type of poison called an **insecticide**. As with herbicides, there are toxic chemicals that can be used as well as some safer, more natural choices.

Keeping good notes. As your garden grows throughout the summer, take notes on what plants and flowers do well and which ones are difficult. Take pictures of your garden and each new plant as it blooms. You might even start your own gardening scrapbook to remember each step of the process.

Plant some annuals, such as marigolds, throughout your perennial garden. Annuals will add bursts of color and fill in any gaps while your perennials are growing. Keep a close eye on your flowers. If they look droopy, they are saying, "Give me some water, please!"

Keeping the plants healthy. One of the most important parts of taking care of your plants throughout the summer is deadheading, or removing old, dried flowers. You can trim off the faded flowers by hand or **ask an adult** to do so with scissors or **pruning shears**. Deadheading helps the plant look better and often grow better. Be sure to wait for the plants to fade on their own before clipping any parts off. Do not clip any new or developing blossoms. Be sure to take off old, dry leaves as well.

Time to Divide

Everything you take the time to do at the end of summer is work you will not have to do the following spring. One of the last steps you can take is dividing up your largest perennial plants. Dividing them will keep them healthier and give them a longer life. Best of all, it will give you more plants to add to your garden—or to give to your friends so that they can start their own garden.

Usually, plants should be divided when they are between two and five years old and have doubled

Garden Tip

An old English saying about perennial gardens states, "First year sleeps, second year creeps and third year leaps." It is the perfect description of how long it takes to get a perennial garden growing.

When you plant
tall plants in the
middle of smaller
ones, they really
stand out.

How to Divide an Iris Plant

STEP 1

Have an adult cut the leaves by one-half.

STEP 2

Use a small shovel or spade to dig up the whole plant. Keep as many roots as you can.

STEP 3

Next, have an adult use a sharp knife to cut the rhizomes into several sections. There should be a group of leaves with each section.

STEP 4

Be careful that the rhizomes do not all point in the same direction. Some should point out. Some should point in. This way the plants will spread out in all directions.

STEP 5

Lay the rhizomes flat. Bury them just below the surface of the dirt. The place where the rhizome meets the first leaves should not be buried. Push down on the dirt firmly. Use your fingers to create an edge all around each rhizome. This makes a bowl to hold water. When you're finished, water each one thoroughly.

or tripled their original size. Some people prefer to divide them in late fall, while others like to wait until early spring. Regardless of when you do it, the process is fairly simple and works for most types of plants:

1. Using a spade or a shovel, dig around the bottom of the plant and carefully, slowly, lift the whole thing out of the soil.
2. Shake or push off most of the soil from the roots with your hand.
3. **Ask an adult** to use pruning shears or a sharp knife to cut apart the healthiest parts of the plant. Most clumps can be separated into four or five sections.
4. Replant each division into a container or into other parts of your garden as soon as possible after the separation.
5. Add two inches of mulch, and then water the plant.

Perennial gardens are lovely—and a lot of fun. They can teach you about everything from weather and nature to responsibility and patience. At the same time, they can make the world a more beautiful place!

Chapter

Chapter

5

Gardening in the City

If you live in an apartment or a place without a backyard, do you have to forget all about growing a perennial garden? Of course not! You can grow some beautiful perennial plants in containers and window boxes.

What kind of containers can you use? You can use anything from traditional clay pots to plastic buckets or even recycled items like old boots or watering cans with holes or cracks in them. There are a few requirements, of course. Make sure the container has proper drainage, a saucer, and enough room for roots.

Wooden containers are fine if they are made out of cedar, cypress, or some other type of wood that does not rot. To help protect the plants from extreme temperatures, you can line the containers with Styrofoam.

Because perennials need warm temperatures, it is important that, if you live in an area that gets quite cold during part of the year, you bring in your containers when winter's chill begins. Inside, some may continue to grow and bloom, while others may go dormant.

Plants that are grown in containers and kept there will need extra care when it comes to watering. They will dry out quicker, depending on the size of the plant, the size of the container, the soil, and the temperature. Watch to see how long your plants can go before

This lovely garden was created by combining potted plants and ground plants. It is a wild mix that makes a peaceful place to spend a summer afternoon.

Almost anything can be turned into a plant container if you just use your imagination. Here an old cowboy boot sports a new paint job and is home to a delicate flower.

starting to droop. Some may need to be watered every few days, and some more than once a day. You can slow down the drying-out process by adding potting soil or wood chips. Be careful not to overwater! Signs that you've given your plants more than they need include

Garden Tip

For many more ideas of what you can add to make your garden extra special, check out Garden Crafts for Kids: 50 Great Reasons to Get Your Hands Dirty *by Diane Rhoades.*

You can plant a large garden, but you might want to keep some of your favorite plants in pots and arrange them in a pretty basket for variety.

Removing the dead or dried leaves and stalks of your plants helps you to see how well they are growing. It is a good way to become familiar with your plants.

white or dark and mushy roots, drooping leaves, and a wet soil surface.

Pruning your container plants is important. Break off any dead or broken stems, leaves, or blooms. This will help your plants stay healthier, look better, and grow stronger.

Although this may sound like a lot of work, it is worth it. Having your own outdoor rainbow is wonderful. Being able to bring it inside with you when the weather turns cold is even better!

Craft

Plant Buddies

To add some extra fun to your garden, especially if it is a small one that sits in a few containers or a window box, why not make some plant buddies? They look cute—and they will keep your growing plants and flowers company!

Things You Will Need

An Adult to Help
Oven
Colorful plastic-coated
    paper clips
Pencil
Several colors of
    modeling clay
Plastic spoon and fork
Cookie sheet
Aluminum foil

Instructions

1. **Have the adult** preheat the oven to 275 degrees.
2. Straighten out a paper clip.
3. Wind the paper clip around a pencil so that it is curly.
4. Pick up a small amount of modeling clay. Hold it in your hand to warm it up, and then begin shaping it into whatever design you prefer. You can make a flower, bee, ladybug, worm,

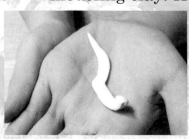

spider, or anything else that sounds like fun to you.

5. Use the plastic fork and spoon to help shape the clay or add lines to your buddy. To make a snake, roll the clay between your hands until it is long and thin. For a caterpillar, make 5 or 6 small balls and push them together. Use your imagination and create whatever you

like the best. There is no right or wrong when it comes to making a craft like this. It is best to keep your buddies, whatever shape they may take, under three inches long so that they will heat up and harden all the way through.

6. When each plant buddy is in the shape you want, stick one end of a curly paper clip into the bottom of it. This is the part that you will push down into the soil.

7. Finally, place your creation on a cookie sheet lined with a piece of aluminum foil. **Have an adult** place the sheet into the preheated oven.

8. Bake for 30 minutes. When the plant buddies are done, **have the adult** take them out. Let them cool for another 30 minutes.

9. Clean up all your supplies.

10. Put your new buddies in your garden!

Further Reading

Books

Alexander, Stephanie. *Kitchen Garden Cooking for Kids.* Herndon, Virginia; Lantern Books, 2006.

Lovejoy, Sharon. *Sunflower Houses: Inspiration from the Garden: A Book for Children and Their Grown-Ups.* New York: Workman Publishing, 2001.

Otten, Jack. *Watch Me Plant a Garden.* New York: Children's Press, 2002.

Snyder, Inez. *Gardening Tools.* New York: Children's Press, 2002.

Winckler, Suzanne. *Planting the Seed: A Guide to Gardening.* Minneapolis: Lerner Publishing, 2002.

Works Consulted

Barash, Cathy. *Perennial Gardens: Great Ideas and Projects for Glorious Color Year after Year.* New York: Better Homes and Gardens, 2001.

Carter, Susan, and Carrie Becker. *Perennials: The Gardener's Reference.* Portland, Oregon: Timber Press, 2007.

Cox, Jeff. *Perennial All-Stars: The 150 Best Perennials for Great-Looking, Trouble-Free Gardens.* Emmaus, Pennsylvania: Rodale Books, 2002.

DiSabato-Aust, Tracy. *The Well-Tended Perennial Garden: Planting and Pruning Techniques.* Portland, Oregon: Timber Press, 2006.

DK Publishing, *Perennials.* London: DK Adult Publishing, 2004.

On the Internet

Backyard Gardener: Perennial Gardening
www.backyardgardener.com/pren/

Colorado State University: Perennial Gardening
www.ext.colostate.edu/pubs/Garden/07402.html

The Helpful Gardener: Perennial Garden Design
www.helpfulgardener.com/perennials/03

Photo Credits: Cover, pp. 1, 2–3, 4–5, 8, 9, 11, 14–15, 17, 20–21, 24, 26, 27, 28, 29, 30–31, 33, 35, 38–39, 40, 41 42—JupiterImages; p. 11 (zone map)—United States Department of Agriculture; pp, 16, 19—Barbara Marvis; p. 25—Amie Jane Leavitt; pp. 23, 43, 44, 45—Tamra Orr.

 Glossary

bacteria (bak-TEE-ree-uh)—Tiny organisms that live in the soil; some are helpful, but others may cause disease.

container (kun-TAY-ner) **planting**—Growing seeds in small containers rather than in the ground.

dormant (DOR-munt)—Inactive or still.

drainage (DRAY-nidj)—The act or process of draining.

fertilizer (FER-tih-ly-zer)—A substance that helps improve the soil.

herbicide (ER-bih-syd)—A substance that kills plants; for use on unwanted types (weeds).

insecticide (in-SEK-tih-syd)—A substance that kills insects.

mulch—A covering of straw, compost, or sheeting that protects the soil around a plant.

nutrients (NOO-tree-unts)—Chemicals that help things grow.

organic (or-GAA-nik)—Compounds that originally came from living plants or animals.

ornamental (or-nuh-MEN-tul)—Used or grown for decoration.

perennials (puh-REH-nee-ulz)—Plants that continue to grow from one year to the next.

pruning shears (PROO-ning sheerz)—Small scissor-like tool used for pruning flowers and shrubs.

rhizome (RY-zohm)—An underground stem that stores food for the plant when the leaves die in winter.

Index